Lad Sees the Vet

By Carmel Reilly

Lad cut his leg.

We got Lad to the vet.

At the vet, Lad can see a big cat.

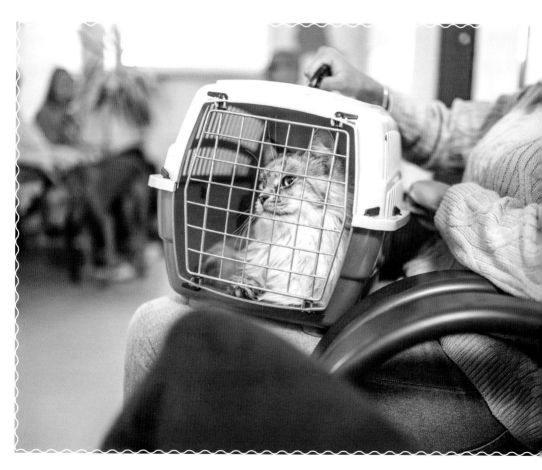

We see a kid and her mum at the vet.

And lots of pups!

We see a hen at the vet, too.

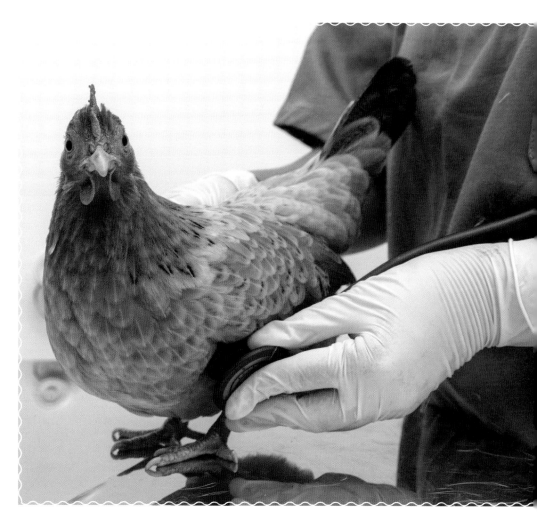

Mum and I got Lad in.

Lad hops up to the vet.

The vet can see the cut.

She gets her vet kit.

Lad had to sit.

The vet said the cut
was not bad.

Lad got a jab.

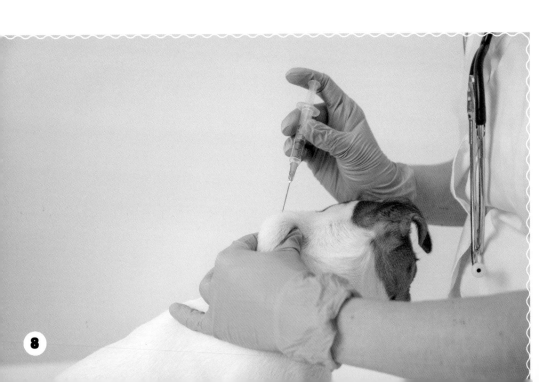

Lad had a sip at a tub.

Lad can go!

CHECKING FOR MEANING

1. Why does Lad see the vet? *(Literal)*

2. What did Lad do at the vet before he was ready to go? *(Literal)*

3. Why do you think the hen was at the vet? *(Inferential)*

EXTENDING VOCABULARY

kit	The word *kit* can mean having the right tools for what you need to do. The vet has a kit in this book. Can you think of another meaning of the word *kit*?
vet	Look at the word *vet*. How many sounds are in this word?
can	Look at the word *can*. What smaller word can you see at the end of this word? What other words do you know that rhyme with *can*?

MOVING BEYOND THE TEXT

1. What do vets do?

2. What other jobs involve helping people or animals?

3. Lad's owners looked after him by taking him to the vet. What else do you need to do to look after a dog?

4. A pup is a baby dog. What other animals have pups? What are some names for different baby animals?

SPEED SOUNDS

Kk	Ll	Vv	Qq	Ww
Dd	Jj	Oo	Gg	Uu
Cc	Bb	Rr	Ee	Ff	Hh	Nn
Mm	Ss	Aa	Pp	Ii	Tt

PRACTICE WORDS

vet

Lad

leg

lots

kid

wag

kit

Wag